Wise Men Seek the Savior

Matthew 2:1–11 for Children

Elena C. Fox

Illustrated by Kate Phillips

CONCORDIA PUBLISHING HOUSE • SAINT LOUIS

In Bethlehem, a mother sits and rocks her baby boy.
This Child was born to save the world and fill our hearts with joy.

She's thinking of the shepherds and the angels that they saw.
The stars are twinkling up above; she gazes down in awe.

Far to the east on this same night, a journey will begin:
For Jesus came for all the world, to take away our sin.

The Wise Men served in kingdom courts and studied all their lives.
They read and learned and knew so much; they watched the earth and skies.

One night, they spied a brand-new star that shined so high above.
They knew it was a sign announcing God's great gift of love.

The Wise Men had been watching for the signs that God would send.
They read the words the prophets wrote: a King would soon descend.

Our sin had kept us separated from our Lord above,
But He sent down a Savior to redeem us with His love.

The Wise Men could not wait another minute in that place.
They headed toward Jerusalem to meet Him face-to-face.

The star continued shining as it led them on their way.
The journey took them many months; they traveled night and day.

At last, they reached Jerusalem; there was no time to lose!
They asked, "Where is the baby born to be King of the Jews?"

The priests and teachers searched God's Word for what had been foretold.
The town of Bethlehem would be the birthplace of the Lord.

The Wise Men thanked them for their help and hurried on their way
To meet the Child of Bethlehem and worship Him that day.

The star they followed went before and led them once again.
And soon it stopped above a house in little Bethlehem.

The Wise Men all were overjoyed to see young Jesus there.
They opened up their gifts of gold and frankincense and myrrh.

They bowed their heads to worship Him and sang to God on high,
Who led them to the King of kings with wonders in the sky.

The journey of these Wise Men happened many years ago,
But Jesus still is with us now, and this we surely know!

So many signs remind us of His presence ev'ryday.
So we can seek and find Him, too, just in a different way.

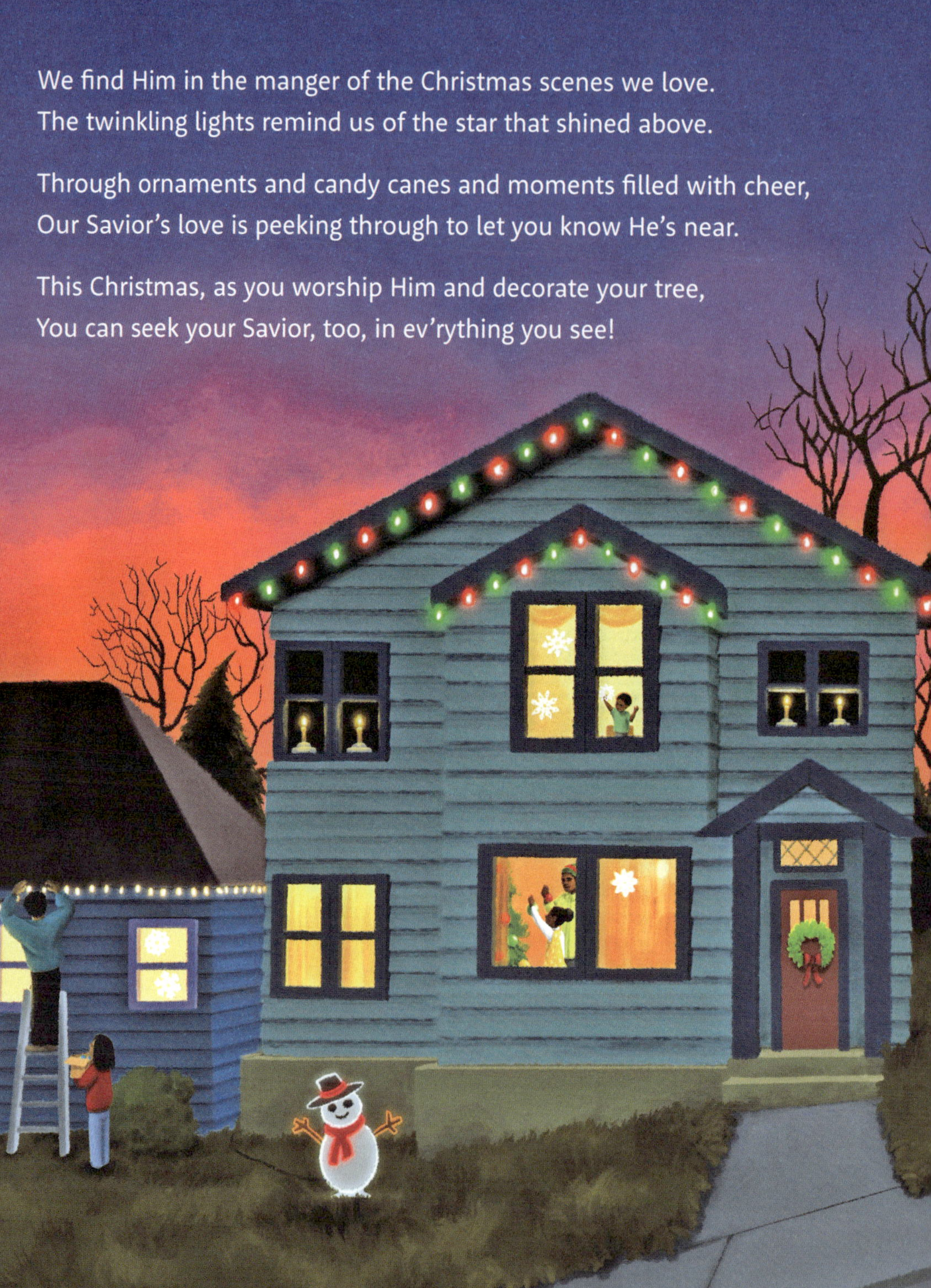

We find Him in the manger of the Christmas scenes we love.
The twinkling lights remind us of the star that shined above.

Through ornaments and candy canes and moments filled with cheer,
Our Savior's love is peeking through to let you know He's near.

This Christmas, as you worship Him and decorate your tree,
You can seek your Savior, too, in ev'rything you see!

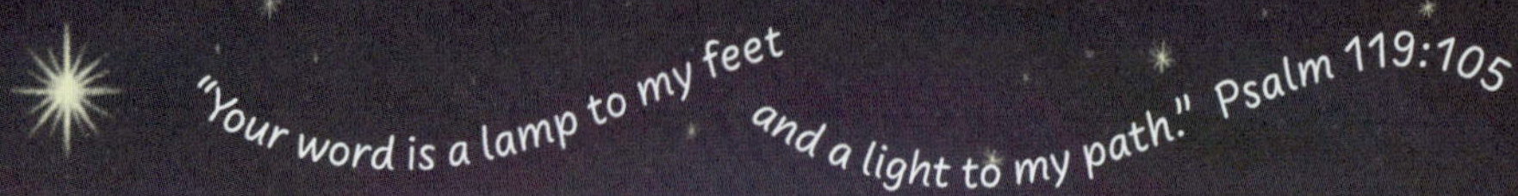

Dear Parents,

The journey of the Wise Men, also known as Magi, that is recorded in Matthew's Gospel is an important moment in the Christmas story. These mysterious men traveled a long distance to worship the Son of God. They were looking for a king, and they found the King of kings. They are the ambassadors for the people of the world. In their story, we are reminded that Jesus came to be the Savior of all, not just of the people of Israel.

The star that guided their journey teaches us something important as well. God uses the signs and wonders of His own glorious creation to reveal Himself to mankind. Because the Wise Men were watching for signs, they were able to stand in the presence of the Savior. But that's not all! They also needed to hear God's Word to know that the King would be born in Bethlehem. God's creation teaches us about Himself, but His Word tells us even more: that Jesus came for the Wise Men and for you!

God still gives us signs to show us His presence in our lives today. After reading *Wise Men Seek the Savior* with your child, point out signs of God's presence in your own Christmas traditions. You can use a nativity set to review the story of Jesus' birth. Let the evergreen branches speak of God's endless love. The colors of the candy cane remind us of the sacrifice our Savior would make on the cross. Bible story books and fun activities remind us of Jesus' love. As you start to look for ways to share signs of God's presence with your child, you may be surprised just how often you will find them. Wise men never stop seeking.

The Author

"His invisible attributes, namely, His eternal power and divine nature, have been clearly perceived, ever since the creation of the world, in the things that have been made."
Romans 1:20